*The Vulnerability
of Order*

The

VULNERABILITY

of ORDER

Martine Bellen

COPPER CANYON PRESS

ACKNOWLEDGMENTS

The author would like to acknowledge the following publications
in which some of these poems first appeared:

Chain, Colorado Review, Conjunctions, Web Conjunctions,
A Convergence of Birds, Crayon, duration, Fence, First Intensity,
Generator, Grand Street, Rhizome, and *Talisman.*

Thanks also to Dim Gray Bar Press, which first
published the chapbook *10 Greek Poems.*

Copper Canyon Press gratefully acknowledges Gregory Crewdson
and Augustine Luhring Gallery for the use of
The Ocean Calls on the cover.

Copper Canyon Press is in residence under the auspices of the Centrum
Foundation at Fort Worden State Park in Port Townsend, Washington.
Centrum sponsors artist residencies, education workshops for
Washington State students and teachers, blues, jazz, and
fiddle tunes festivals, classical music performances, and
The Port Townsend Writers' Conference.

LIBRARY OF CONGRESS CATALOGING-IN-PUBLICATION DATA

Bellen, Martine.
The vulnerability of order / Martine Bellen. — 1st ed.
p.   cm.
Poems
ISBN 1-55659-157-8 (alk. paper)
1. Title.
PS3552.E5336 V8 2001
811'.54 — DC21
2001002047

3 5 7 9 8 6 4 2
FIRST PRINTING

COPPER CANYON PRESS
Post Office Box 271
Port Townsend, Washington 98368
www.coppercanyonpress.org

for Bradford

Contents

SOJOURNER TRUTHS

NINE GREEK
POEMS

for Guy Davenport

Perennials

First aria
In open field

Bulbs bloom, come crocus,
Nexus viola, trillium

Look to the bow and lyre
How opposing forces agree

Moon poppies backdrop
A carpet of columbine

Symphytum spoon spread
Red in bed of pink then cream

Variegate color and bass
Ah, the blues, the *blues.*

Cuccina

I.

The most beautiful order is still
A random collection
Of things insignificant in themselves:

II.

Cranberry rosettes and candied
Violets, frosted thumb plums
Sweating midday, and gingerbread
Shaped in stars and bells.

III.

A buck, doe, and fawn dunk
Apples down near the pond where
Blue heron stalks rainbows
That dart while light recedes.

IV.

Under feather comforters and tea-rose vaults,
We sleep smelling of last night's
Spices. Outside, trees shed quilted leaves.

For the Saturday Evening Girls' Pottery Club

Please, oh please, spread something sweet
Over my shredded wheat

That rests upon this yellow plate,
Fired in its biscuit state.

Mystic swastika hands abound,
Fortune, luck, well-being found,

And bowls with bands of ducks
And trees, ring around the ABCs.

Hand-thrown pots incised in ink;
Still-soft clay, initials sink.

Please, today, come sip some tea
With small designs, each cup's *jolie,*

The harmony lies not in line
But deeper in the object's rhyme.

White Butterfly

If every butterfly were smoke, would all perception
Fall to smell? If every wing were paper-white, would

All perception end in sight?
Stitch of Michelin lace or brood of Phoebus Parnassian.

This subarctic gossamer,
Kaleidoscopic absence absorbs alpine stonecrop

Across sage flats
Tundra

And bleeding
Hearts. She escapes the loose cocoon

In grass tussocks which protect.
And evaporates before a gust.

To Etienne Silhouette

The shadow-machine scales

                One's profile

By our adjusting flame

             And sitter —

                    A most diminutive way

Of keeping loved ones.

            For without opposition

All things cease

          To be

Seen. How a star collapsed

             Bends light

Until invisibility

           Is achieved. The shade cutter knows

This, as she reduces portrait

              Into warring essence —

White against black

          Absence defining shape —

The silhouette enlarged on scrim

                Taunting us

Awaiting capture.

Swifts and Swallows

Sparrow-sized swallows swoop
Insects, peck bayberries. An aberrant
Of notes and dives. Though incomplete

Breastband may confuse a tree
Swallow with a rough-winged,
The voice, *weet, trit, weet,*

Not a harsh *trrit,* rougher
Than the bank swallow's *trr-tri-tri,*
Should clarify, for those who wish to know the world

Must learn it from its detail,
Its swallowlike swifts, with illusory wing,
Alter a twinkle and glide.

All Beasts Are Driven to Pasture

Buddha Bear, sea lion on surface, sleeps in the sink,
Slinks under city drainpipes. But weekends allay

Hibernation of the vestigial tiger, and the Buddha
Rubs snout to grass, limb extends limb. Stalks

Deer and wild turkey. Devours flying dragons.
Bottled in muscle for flight, my beast chases bee up a tree.

Herbal Wisdom

The kingly *basilikon* must be reviled,
Spit upon, abused for abundance
Tho admixed with goose grease so good
For babies' ears and aphrodisiacs.

"Ego, Borago, gaudia semper ago."
The oxtongue's liquid quiets
A wildman but combined with wine
One howls and pines. "I,
Borage, always give courage."

Who said character is fate?
I should like to sate
Myself with sage and thyme.

The Circle's Beginning

Our bed – a wall on which salvages cast
"Job's Troubles" or "Crazy"

Which means *random* in quilting.

Stretchers suspend space
And women side by side

Practice stitchery

To protect loved ones
From the cold.

Thousands of pieces

Applied to form
A whole that cures

Our bed – a wall on which salvages cast
The beginning or end of a circle.

ON THE PATH
TO MIND PALACE

The Vulnerability of Order

for Elaine Equi

Caves, here, *contain dead/live*
snakes, some keys, for instance,
have holes or   ,
the transgressive guardian, mind
with wings beneath.

She felt the urge to send musk-confects,
Across the Strait of Gibraltar

Interior, private floods, neshamah (Jewish soul),
food with cinnamon curry,

Here, sea-goddess hosts aquatic monsters,
Traipse rabble of spooks
& devil's marionette. She attends lectures on anatomy,

Explores the yolk sac, our centerpiece,
Primitive heart. *Her*

Secret breath sounds the confident demons
Attune
      atonement
              a vowel an opening to the divine

God resides in the odd
Clamor, the *Ein Sof*

Female indwelling (pre-séance)
Oldest mystery of my ear
Opening the door   *shutters*   where message is married

Wind between heaven &   , word & lip
      Lived both forward and compassion *om mani padme hum*
How moment follows movement

She is *bemidbar* or in the desert
With *bubbe meise* (a grandmother tale)
Law without vowel
Rooking planet-strooken

      For this woman, paralyzed and word-full,
      Chained to a mobile home with its process narrative,
      God is the one who counts
      Numbers, days, seductions, bones

      Inscribed in body. Outside
      She's drowning, weeping,
      Will stop at nothing for time.

Her voice, the wandering part of her flesh
In the Old/New Synagogue
                        In parchment, in hieroglyph.

Nocturne

The Swan sails a milky tide spread evenly across *Silver River*
& Pierrette angry with the moon and universe of flute, viola, harp
Harmonizing our corrupt selves with the utterly impassible
Unable to suffer
Without leitmotiv

Not to denote absence but to describe in negative terms to
     capture the fades and sequences

The equation of peering at the sky upside down, at Cassiopeia,
     a sequin,
Butterfly's dream, Andromeda
                   Philosophical toys contenting
                      emblematic identity

Below her waist: blue coral

    Cloud's breath root-coiled to earth
    How matter's faithless

    Miscellaneity under a simmering cinder moon
    Omen of bones, ignoble, central moods

    Crinkum-crankum frogs congesting trees
    Shaded by a turbid glow

    Bee's familiarities
    With the mild moon

Key to the bright world

Communal & personal aspects of integrating with sound as
      landscape
(*converted luminosity*)

She sleeps in black-and-white woods,
Only when awake do colors saturate
Habitats of resonance
Glass splashed with spells, *canciones*

Ghouls, fouler wind, and swollen waves
                    A passing moon, passion moon

The sword which lies ready for battle in the open heart, shiny moon
      (A hidden moon scuds behind broken cloud)

Or is the Divine Window — apprehension of our invisible body
Tucked away in the prose closet
Neck-ruffles of stars and the *dones d'aigo*
Sheltered in underground waterfalled halls, weaving water
To gowns, the living mutable spirit of each fountain:
      The Tender Fount, Coarse Spring,
            Spring of Deceit, Glassy Fountain,
                  The Dried-up Spring
(*reduce amount of blood in body, reduce desire*)

Innermost subtle drops
                    Suffusing throat, heart

Gave speech to bird and wind
That dance for an audience of one; still swirls
Of bejeweled tulle pirouette in echoing applause,
Like the clinks of cordial glasses
Inspiriting the dark alone

She is an idiot, walks through the burden forgetting
What disappeared. Her
                    World fell away. A wind, hitherto unknown,
                        physically unanimous,

All the Devils of Hell cannot pluck a feather from one poor wren.

Meditations on Falling Past

I.

You who have gone into the grave
A carved D — Duration's tongue
Pushing off the roof of your mouth

Letting
            The ghetto torn

                  Torah   agate

            glass

Light resurrecting Lazarus

II.

Rag- and fog-junkman with prayer candles
Clashing chants, crowned
Humiliation, pride
                        imprisoned

III.

        As Sabbath soul abandons
Soil,

Father
            The wanderer, Jew,

Walking backward

                                        — slice of pipe
Just desserts

        — object and instrument of objection

When it's removed: the anima. loss of an eye.
                                        omens or

        — there, there

                        ——

        Bodies piled twelve deep
                        Pebbles atop tombstones

                        ——

CREATION OF A DEMAND SATISFIED

You speak of love as an example...

        (& exile as desertion)

Underground tunnels through fog
and frogs swallow their skin, through night
webs, honey, orbs
of echoes, padlocked doors

a hierarchy of deceptions

confound me in a cave, my flesh its walls

Interlinear vision
              interior
                        beef tears

I of the It

Formhood, how death confines
                   found me

Polluted my sleep

A spell of separation

———

Too quick for me to weary
            You sing an electric spark

———

PROTECTION OF IMPRESSIONS

I.

Although translucence
won't claim permanence

what we fear can be
seen though

encountered unrecognizable
— disfigured, deteriorate

a quorum wailing the Kaddish
lost entrance of a transcendental

home — amorphously small, sense
of smell, weight, the sentence

received, not experienced
but a presence, it presents itself

a self, which doesn't
pertain to self, what does?

II.

Of unrelated hours
described by the Memorialists

straw pillows
excogitated center
anterior collective ends

anus mundi — worms in woman's hair

———

Sacral dance or moon
At the bottom of the puddle

Perfumerie

Aleph is heard (a *silent* letter) &
Maggid [storyteller] sings in the language of green salt [bitter
    herbs, mortar]
      Seven stories of sin
           Each striating the next
Holy opening

Form for story's outline, flavor in separate packets for content

Doorsill

A holy soup

Still

Between gates, memories so circuitous and windows filled with
night, disappearing houses, underpinnings of articulation, while
in the rewritten text one's life has to be surrendered or bluebottle
flies, those preemptive pallbearers, strew death Hermetic tension.

Remains.

No love lost between the soul & body

Scriptural sorrow as blind bless
The moon, invisible to them. Quietism.

    (As Buddha can't see water, yet dunks)

(*The creator* his creation, yet grieves)

Fidelity to the instant discourages/incurs miracles,
                                    (disrupter of expectations;
                                        hope, our humidifier)

Impassive intensities.

Reticent

What hides behind the guise of complexity?

Utterance

Impermanence of the knower reflects the permanence of
    knowledge.
Such is the light which never dims as it travels from its source

To source   a transference chain   train of soil   soul   to source

From seeing   to shiny
To sea

Five names for the soul

        could be mistaken for content, loins for form

The lawless mind, changeling

As it's designed. Splitting line from mass.

                    each ruling a different entrance

Sliver through to nonland. First glow or
Exquisite spirits
Quivered escapes.

Magic Musée

for Joseph Cornell

I.

She, who's overconscious of her cage
Formed from heat, moisture, frost, concealment,

How it drips, freezes, fogs
How it forms columnar cracks gashed with glass

Toward the blue peninsula, gravity flight
The visible half of reflection

Attempting to obtain the solidity of an object

Or to remove the clothing of sound, genealogical anxiety,
Disrobing at the Hotel Eden

Inventing a way in
To that which is built over concept

II.

Behold, Thoreau sings for owls; Dickinson, hummingbirds
Still life enframes world of spectacle

Or object-spirits

Dewish   mute

The Pyramids are letters, some die inside
Cul-de-sac feelings, or Stonehenge numbers
In twilight the lamp illumines ideological will

A weaving of walls, movable wicker
& caravan carpets strung twixt reeds
Our ground breathes, floats, as we wander
Into cosmologies, cosmogonies
Immeasurable emblems of circumference or protractor

III.

She developed the disease of demonic enthusiasm
On looking at a nymph,
Mystic hunt through childhood, *histoire* of fountains
Dominating the *jardin* canary parasols
Perpetual noon antipasto sun *crème* ballerina
Idyllic dying swan

IV.

Wire-netted cage papered with constellations
Promises of progress or unfoldment from her magic prison
She traces an analemma, her eyes infinitely distant,
Maps night sky or soap bubbles
Navigated by songbird
Whose droppings streak the air
Reminiscent for us of a comet's tail
The result of yesterday's path-strewn birdcrumbs

V.

Occupants of the *Étrangers*
Exalted chanters with a self-contained view
Small white frame

Moon
Sustained patterns of meaning

Spindly-armed shadows stretch through lace curtains
Historians of the mind's voyage

As with other repressions, a vestige of the animal within
Seamless continuum, therefore the bordertown Nostalgia

Her liquid limbs, she interior
To the melody alone

Unraveled eveners

Foaming grottoes & feathered
Lures — yearnings of detachment
Symbolized and effected

Travelogue of a faun's dream

The Science of Mixtures

We are in a glorious era of Chemistry.
Let's ponder its chimeric properties!

In scarlet chambers
A vaporous state
Vowel plainsong

This molecular transference of energy
Issues forth & capable
Of assuming multitudes of forms without suffering
Alteration.
Such quality necessary
To see

(sleeper's crawl-space)
Pretend element

(remove light from fire)

Icicles suffer crystals
lungs in Siberia
brows in Jamaica
Cold narcosis/
Owes its pleasant fresh taste to air

Chrysalis of Arctic-blue butterfly

I. THE HISTORY OF BURNING BODIES

Intimately connected to that on which it acts — Two bodies selfless,
Of different temperatures, combine honey-blood treacle

Laws of heat's language analogous to those of motion,
Tulip-dance   *Dido, Jeanne d'Arc, Hansel's witch,*

Particles excite cold in surrounding areas,
Between confinement & liberty,

Stimulate   given space   graven
                 Afterbirth   Air/Earth

Sprites pass through petals
Large columns blue

Coagulated light, full of winds and meteors, tosses our globe,
Common air yields to the slightest impulse,

Wounds, stamens
Wind speed

II. HYBRIDIZATION

Part flautist, part pipit,
Part pea, our divining daykeep
Fleeces sound from fire,
Terrestrial/celestial, expires
Aurora borealis.

She appears volatile or fugitive
A spontaneous doppelgänger replaces
Her last seconds, concrete
Found in the heart, a dead-white color

Instead of feet, fins
 instead of fins, wings

Song of the Little Road

after Satyajit Ray

Characters

Apu — boy of six
Durga — girl of eight
Auntie — "Father's" mother, old bag of bones
Oaf
Mother — disillusioned
Father — impotent
same ol' same ol'
Neekamel — God
Fruit has no name on it
Learning to love generously

    Bamboo birds and girls in gardens
Oil, salt, chilies stolen from the kitchen

like a fork in the road

the orchard is private property

AUNTIE: Must I ask for chilies & guava at my age?
        And anyway, fruit has no name on it.

The candyman always wants
more than the sweets he offers

He promotes desire, discord
with his halvah and fudge

Mother drags daughter
by her beautiful mane
beads and seeds fall from her
magic box — cowries

      inadmissible
           desire
               dying's
      the easy part
      like shutting off the projector and sitting in the dark

Afterward brother finds her
precious booty. Neekamel keeps guard.

MOTHER: This home is like living in the forest!
          No one to talk to.

We stop looking
At the other

      APU: There's a ghost in the water.

This is about monsoons
    towels
    her seeds
    buttons

     his

  sex

Sometimes it's necessary to leave home.

Devi

Turn back, return
one thousand years, twist
her curved back, carved sandal-
wood hips, till time takes her

subtle body between states achieved by accelerated deaths

into the Dance of Kali.
Space shivers. Siva. Was his face
blue? or did her eyes catch
the ocean in a filament of rippling skin?

———

The sky, no longer beyond our grasp but an interior
    composition,

with color, too   foam
    and many preservers — Vishnu, Parvati, Durga

foreboding as any keep, craving, enchanted weapon

———

Pelicans, flamingos, herons — the *mantig a tayr* (language of birds)
language of escape. An elegy is the bond between air and breach,
                    a released energy
the loosed verve of devotion

The hidhid,

A tree gracious enough to lend its name to the mountain that
    houses its roots

    Wind scuttling leaves is an elegy
    Birdsong: an elegy
    Ring of holy chants

———

    Devotion: repeating a practice
    without repetition,
                    devotee,
                            Devi,
                                votive

    A fifth world war fought outside time
    Mind part battlefield:

Unborn   enduring   indestructible   embodied   inspirit

What dissolve are the ordinary aspects —
The ghosting roots of an ash,
    A butter-lamp,
        Intestinal garlands,
    Lands that lack volume.

This is autumn

Smells of sun and mums rise from spindly grass

If matter and energy are equivalent and light
the manifestation falls between,

       space between her teeth
                            She sings scales

a breeze gathers synergy

said to affect the Pacific Ocean,   (specific) opens her mouth

                           Universe of names

Elegies for indigo and saffron leaves,
rain pounding rock. Reedy notes immerse
lichen, all variety of fern and fearful creature.

Look! Two birds in the tree, one eats, the other regardeth only.

———

A last scream lingers like the mocking of brilliance
from an extinguished star she preys on.
Midnight breeze caresses her.
(She cannot dance it, laden with apples,
popsicles, obstacles.) Her spine
visited by Shakti
                    from the forehead of Durga

                         her most terrible aspect,

circling the throat and sex
with Kiki's glass sperms, skulls, with fury.

No rationale for this natya
of shattered aura, shattered faith

Sadhana   (practice) forges the heart
     the jiva and atman. One bird eats; the other, a witness

     dresses of Prada scarves of Chanel

                    ———

Where Sound corresponds to creation,
Hear Great Vac's drum, the goose lives
In the Himalayan's shadow, pilgrim soul
Takes flight toward columns of continuum —

Composed of sand, saffron threads, unexcelled
Wisdom, wind or mirrors,
    Our protective circles

    Oceanic volcano throat
    Opens a word disturbs
    The deep prana

Scarves of rustling light

Foundation Mandala

for Claire

Of sapphire. Systematically construed
off a square; offering
deities a balcony on which to dance

How does one illuminate the atmosphere?

  Sheath of candles
  Irrigate the four winds

Ganesa round back repairs walls
while the girl maps elements of philosophy
and posthumously eavesdrops on Grandmother
whose files, over six feet thick,
contain wisdom applicable to Vermeer, birds, *fabula,*
penny arcades, and the chance encounter
of a sirocco and softened laughter.

The girl disguising herself as an old spider
in a thirteenth-century limnal magic lantern
exacts impulses from light and pearls of moisture
which accumulate on complex webbing
as Picasso eats cats,
woos & plays the flute.

  This boundless structure binding structure,
  city of flesh and bones

Hear white wheat
where mind drops, a vibrant precipice

Indra inspects the floors of the building,
consults diagrams drawn in mineral on brocade,
tests supports, balance, flexibility.

    Holiness as a star,
              octagon, circle, jewel

        Traditionally sand-painters applied this city
        of shadow, channels, culs-de-sac,
        moving inward toward its heart

Trappings of misknowledge in Grandma's cabinets
the girl uses to reconstruct conditions of weather,
directional colors, the need of her being in her need
to escape, she pirouettes atop the head of a pin,
petals of tears and pomegranate minaret. My lost ballerina
sloshes ringside the spectral world held in place by neural wind
where everyone has two names, lives according to the outer
universe or train's harmonic connection to its crossing

        drywall, five transparent layers
        of panisks, dakini, guardian dragons

Consecration of this mandala eliminates reversals,
a frameless forest from throat to heart,
in ornamental buildings with indelible arms
to carry and heal when embraced.

        Tinkling bells announce transition of natural phenomena

SOJOURNER
TRUTHS

Belle Starr

Belle, wake up
Her cheek resting on the icy pond

Shadow of a thug turkey-shot her
in the back, neck, and breast
Colt tore through her face

Her last bath
in turpentine and crimson cinnamon
Pallbearers dangle six-shooters

Corn bread in the coffin
Wake up, Belle

On the other side the bread was ett
her outlaw in-laws provended.
A smile welds those wire lips
under wired lids — black
beaded eyes, a sky
on ceiling tacked, another world.
Only it is opposite,
so when she dies here, she finds her hope,
hemp-rope holding all in place
with peckish ravens darting back and forth.

Father was an innkeeper. We called him
Judge for his sternness and popularity.

(He locked her in
his closet, to keep her
his Confederate virago.)

A wingbeat

the haunts the hurts, ball and chain.

In dream you crackle like ice over earth
like lust against the plains.

As a child, to harbor a secret
lands you in bondage;
then, as a woman, outlaws
harbor in your heart and land

Belle a born uglee

Eyes evolved not
because of mind's need to see —
but neurons must preexist
with a light sensitivitee

———

Cherokee sun is she

Down Dallas way she's
The Bandit Queen,
Queen of the Outlaws,
Long velvet train
Riding her stallion Black Venus
Down the main

Faro table, whiskey up, and those
Jolly lads, Southern night riders

While Jim was out, a scout
For the next crime scene

Nesters, squatters, shooters
Who'd disarm or arrest her?

Who'd undress her?
A .45 under her skirt.

Word has it the Tumbleweed Wagon rolls
and gangs travel, wheat in the wind.
The iron-rimmed-wheel prison
wields fear from afar where humans
like hounds armed to the teeth
are shackled in irons and washing
the dishes and fighting
fires that burn through the prairies.

When Belle and Sam Starr were apprehended
on a horse-stealing charge, she tossed out
the blankets, the pots and the pork,
the stove, and the fork. So the marshal tossed
Belle on the cold metal floor with rebuke.

That year, she fixed 'em a grand supper of rattlesnake stew.
And coffee like glue.

Rolled on the floor as they puked.

Yes, the Petticoat of the Plains, dare-may-care. She rolled
on the floor as they puked. Thus, outlaws sought her advice.

She, their Guiding Spirit, gave chase
In black invisible

Wound in a buckskin
Of rattlesnake rattlers

Up north the Hi-Early Mountains
Far west a cranberry sunset
The earth on Cherokee Nation

Only approach to her cabin
Was through a narrow canyon

Fortlike with fine furniture
Famed for its Hawkins's Portable Grand,
And its Belle Starr Creek

She washed her feet and raised
Her girl Pearl to be a lady

Coarser variations of air produce sound

Stillwater Penitentiary

Released on bond and a shopping spree

Each husband shot, replaced

She could read the wanted posters
on each face

Their obituaries
she could read

———◆———

With the grace of a cat
the Colt left his holster

Velvet sky
Moon on high
Last star seen

Lola Montez

How we jump
         Over the moon
      Spirit of entry
                  Ecstasy

———

She
was not
willing to part
with what
she was
who she is and that explains how
she became the way she was

and that explains
how she became
the way
she
looked

Pour over pallor
handfuls of jasmine, rose
petals, and water from orange.
Strain through porous purple paper.
Add a scruple of musk, of ambergris.

    (*The Arts of Beauty* by L. Montez)

   Pure transparent
   layer over paler blue.
   Hair a hollow tube
   filled with fluid.

To prevent fluid from turning
gray an old Gibraltar actress
used the following preparation:

Oxide of bismuth .... 4 drs.
Spermaceti .... 4 drs.
Pure hog's lard .... 4 oz.

   (*The Arts of Beauty; Or, Secrets of a Lady's Toilet*)

Melt lard and spermaceti.

    Become willing
     to part
     with
    what you are

Who was Lola Montez?

Lieutenant's Wife, Danseuse, Lola of the Parisian Coterie,
Courtesan, Mistress of the King of Bavaria, Countess of
Landsfeld, Lola as Exile and Catalyst of Revolution, Coronet
Heald Misses, Bigamist, Pioneer, Mrs. Partrick Hull, Lola
Lecturer, Authoress, Spiritualist, Religionist.

Of which Lola do you speak?

Dies 17 January 1861, New York City. Tombstone reads
    Eliza Gilbert.

Coal color Dolores
lover Dumas
namesake mistake
lover Liszt
listless Dolores cold
Bavarian cream

Vivat Lola!
Pereat Lola!

La Montez
mammon

Lolaministerium
revolution hysterium
macaroni and Brie

Vivat Lola?
Pereat Lola?

If the elbow is a king
King Ludwig of Bavaria
a grass ingredient

The Bohemian Countess of Landsfeld
Vivat

TWO PANTOMIMES

THE SPIDER DANCE

One becomes an abundance
She shakes from her skirt

Her bodice transforms, sweet
Andalusian invaded by Jesuits

Limitless space in her limbs
Hips limit space, wave wider and wilder

Hundreds of wire spiders
Snap in her castanets

The viewer wishes to unravel her
Segmented divisions, inamorata

An erratic course that holds your noblesse

The erotic irradiates off her petticoats
Stamps each to death

LOLA AND HER TROUPE OF DANCING GIRLS, ALL UNMARRIED, MOST UNDER SIXTEEN

Lola Montez plays La Montez
An exact *replica of her Munich Barerstrasse*

Scene I: Lola with lace and mantilla. Ticktack of *taconeos*.
Fandango heat. Whorls in flame. Her alabaster skin soaked.
La Dame Danseuse.

Act II: In toque with tricolor cockade,
buckle, and sash, marcel curls, the Politician in Lola
signs writs, feeds her subjects cake
while Lola the Countess entertains Nobles and
Notables, the Revolutionist Lola through
Bavarian streets stabs
Jesuits, as the Fugitive suffers alone in her castle.
Her disillusionment
Their jealousy.

The Final Vision: Lola abandoned yet strong. Diffuse light
projects from behind. Then, one by one, each
character returns, bows before her,
declares love, begs forgiveness:
Ludwig I, Dujarier, Captain Lennox...

She accepts their hands

Ends in a minuet.

When the chest sways gracefully on the firmly poised waist,
swelling in healthy and noble expanse, then the mind is at its
peak. We are now ready to expand civilization and lure men into
performing acts of greatness. Does the end justify the means,
you ask? Oh, do not be a silly. Those that are cruel, and many
of them there are, call me an opportunist, but quite the contrary,
I am a spiritualist, believe that all matter can transform when
properly instructed.

Lola Montez' Lectures on Beautiful Women

Her cellar stored strange spirits:

von Bülow and bullterriers
Sketches by Boz and Lord Byron's *Don Juan*
a brown bear chained to her garden gate
perched parrot — memento mori
yards of velvet, guipure, and satin
tarts and tartine, dog whips and whip cream
Tartarus and temper
lectures on temperance
rogues and rouge, stays and stiffs
laments and lifts
rare roses aplenty in bottles of crystal
quinces and capers
luxuriant whiskers
mistakes in the dark
tongues wagging briskly

"Can forget my French,
but can't forget my Christ," says
Lola the Penitent.

Outcast creatures
asylumed she tours
with Jesus.

Bereft of beauty, riches,
love and faith prepare
the flesh.

Cradled by
His will
Lola falls asleep.

Lola the Penitent
with Jesus
her flesh falls.

At first it's warm.
Deeper down, the more
forgotten, how chilly
and lost I am
to the surface.

I'll stay here.
Perpetual voice and
motion vanquished.
Last night was years ago
when I lectured on beauty.

We laugh of it, ephemeral vanities
produce pain, somewhere. Who have I wounded
not yet born? A casing that
takes my soul and burns

In the sun. To remove a tan,
die; *crème de l'enclos,* the enclosure,
I advise in my pamphlet — a coffin will do the trick.

H.P. Blavatsky

Mongolian Isis eyes
Ice and flame spine
Rise into the horizon
Mahatma's life zone

Her body a warehouse
Noise, stored memories
And when they're released
Astral minerals disclose

A symphony of sound we are
Unaware the adept's secret
Thought polaric
Suspense
Suspend
Disbelief

She studies strange books
Great-granddad, Prince Pavel

Left behind, esoterics
Of night riders & brigadiers

Masons & Rosicrucians
Occult orders, forces

Momentarily explicated

Transmigrating through the Sahara Desert
An avatar of ancestors

Acting from within — the moral reflection
In a mirror of inner condition

Immortal monad
Human language absorbed

A soundless sleep
Individuals unite in Absoluteness

Om, seed syllable or impersonal personal
In nessness I nest. We Meet.

Brotherhood
Of Luxor. Egyptian.
Cabala. Letters appeared
From the Mahatmas — Master
Morya and Master Koot Hoomi

Electrically an overflow
Of changes. We align into
Self — grand, divine wisdom — *theosophia*.
Mystical alphabets precipitate psychically

Found
In crannies and nooks
In a brother's hand
Spiritual status
Symbol

Through Russia, Allahabad, Darjeeling
On foot through Greece, Egypt, Caicos by caravan,
Obese and in black through Burma, Java, Canada,
For *Maha,* magic — the great well

Passed Germany, Turkey, Italy, she obfuscates
Her path on paper — halved moons of Tibet, Kashmir, Rockies

Soul escapes near Cairo, Ceylon, England
The lodger strides inside her through Damascus, Odessa, and on

Edison was a Theosophist
knitting light into bulbs.

Lucifer, London's magazine carried
harmony. We fold back

into life — reincarnate, captive
in form

Everything follows law
visible or indwelling,

the triune Nature
of Man

Master's about us
dictating destiny

Mongolian Isis, she
spins spines.

Where phantom
Forms solidified

Séances drew us
To a Vermont farm

So many soulless creatures,
Wander our United States, simulacra

Of men and women, their residua,
Our passions controlled passively,

The plastic nature of will; she had
Called them out — a Mussulman from Tiflis,
Kurdish cavalier, the Caucasus servant,

Envelopes of what once were
Spirited lives now spooks.

We are the dead-and-gone people.

On the eve
of an amputation
He cures her
with a white dog's lick

Adyar,
India, a year past
her death, so many
lotuses did float.

Pocahontas

Too far away to be
Seen singly, they come

Together. The coat-wearing
People. They come

On floating isles. Carry
Thunder sticks. They look

For back seas where clove
And mulberry grow. They come

From beyond the great ocean.
With a cross God

They come.

Her first English word was "jewel."

As the sun rose, Ahone took the stream water
off her body and she was one, cool and sparkling.

Mocha brow. Wide-lipped fauna, mutant birds,
water monkeys, and other delights sketched in oyls

on her legs and arms. Maybe ten when she cartwheeled
past his men, proud of her strength, a wilde girl.

Bid Pokahontas bring hither　　*Kekaten pokahontas patiaquagh*
two little Baskets, and I will　　*ningh tanks manotyems*
give her white beads　　　　　*neer mowchick rawrenock audowgh.*
to make her a chaine.

Hither she ran, and round
her neck a circle of light

Language and desire
to understand magic

the other possessed the other's
country a half each didn't know

This priest of paper　　　　　　　　　This stranger
conveyed truth　　　　　　　　　　　from nothing
when he sent a word　　　　　　　　　lives outside
without his body　　　　　　　　　　　　fear

distance
between
as sea
and land unite
in the state of flesh

If not for the daughter
Who durst not be seene
Cheek streaked
Trader

Hidden under
Heathen moon

Wilde traine
Berry juice and bloodroot
Through irksome woods
I will keep my promise
In exchange for some peeces, a cock, and hen

Love you not me?
Deep in Powhatan territory

Pocahontas:

Baptized Rebecca the Lord Jesus
loves me, but at night, with shoes removed,

my toes still smell of our Algonkian ground,
and wise ancestors visit and whisper our secrets.

Small skins I leave for laughing Ahone
who tickles my soles. And though Father could not agree

to all their demands they would have permitted
my return but soon I met John Rolfe,

farmer of the esteemed weed, and after moments
realized I found the stranger in myself.

A marriage between two hemispheres.

Tomocomo:

Powhatan orders to know the number of men
    in this England, but many exist
        as leaves or grains of sand, too infinite
            to count. Here, soil abandons earth.
                These explorers of liquid-ground who sail air.

The Daughter, in whalebone,
    dresses as these people
        and so does her son, the next chief
            who will always smell
                a foreign beast even to himself.

He will step atop a house, walk on their cloud.
    When I stepped off the *Treasurer,*
        onto Plymouth, my dreams
            shrank smaller than what they've created.

        I am diminished.

John Smith:

Eight years since we last met, and cry
she did upon seeing me whom she thought

dead. Worse behaved Christens
I have met. She nineteen, a mother,

colonist. God must have helped in her conversion,
like any young lady, upon the settee she sat.

Yet all I had taught
her and she me,
how our hands felt, fell
to our sides, as language failed.

Pocahontas, first Native American
to die on foreign soil. She left us a son,
inheritor of her
mother's land.

Isabella

Slave
Freedman
Saved
Free Soul

First birth I was a twinkle
Faithful Isabella, first

Birth deep earth uneven
And ungrounded light

Cannot fall, Father was tall, called
Baumfree or low Dutch for tree.
Mother, Mau-Mau Bett. Sweet.

I remember thee as shade
And sun, sold as sheep

Jesus, where were you
When my parents cried?

Mau-Mau showed
Her children a moon,
His light
Bathed their minds,
Their souls
Knew possession

no one can see / how I should be /
the bonehouse is where I want to flee / where no one
can whip me / No One with your omniscient eyes /
leave my body / allow transcendentality

Pipes we smoke and plant 'round pits
Fly into Heaven — a breath from God
Graves scattered with shells, glass, flashes
For quick travel to safety, the sacred

Holy Wind of Whitsuntide

As a woman
She smoked
A small clay pipe

Fella say, no unclean
Thing can enter
The Kingdom of Heaven,
And you with that
Smoker's breath ain't.

Says Truth, "When I go,
I 'spect to leave my breath behind."

Was the ringing bell of Hardenberg
Was a twinkle — Isabella

Memory and orality
Visionary literacy

I told Jesus it'd be all right
If He changed my name

Mauled so badly by a mob
Walked life with a cane

Sojourner Truth I became

Visionary memory
Amanuensis or numen

Where narrative is silent

Her song, strong truthful tones

In the cellar of her birth
Baumfree and she
Exchanged
Their last *thought*
No longer than a finger

"I am colored, thank God for that;
I have not the curse of God upon me."

On a small island in a small stream
Speaking loudly as her breath blew
Willows   silver falls

Insurrection   carry off

Her cries to God

June 1: The clarion blows
East from Brooklyn to Long Island
"Lord giveth me a new home.
I must be about my Father's business."

Dusts off her traveling shoes, loads up
Some *cartes de visite;* her *Narrative;*
And an album for autographs —
The "Book of Life."

> *It was early in the morning,*
> *It was early in the morning,*
> *Just at the break of day,*
> *When He rose, when He rose, when He rose,*
> *And went to Heaven on a cloud.*

And trees wave in glory
Stones shine like laughter
And she shouts "Praise to the Lord
Love to all creatures!"

In Quaker garb
Stands six feet
Tall lean royal
Sibilla Libica

Chin rests on
Broad hard palm
Eyes bespeak
Power to bind

In portraiture Sojourner reclines,
Lincoln above. The "Book of Life" open.

Six months later, our President dead

In truth, Lincoln's seated at his desk when Sojourner
Arrives. He stands and bows upon introduction.

He says: All presidents would have emancipated
          those brought in bondage *if the time had come,*
          and if those on the other side of the river
          had not done evil, I wouldn't have had
          the opportunity to do good.

An instrument of God

Both hands receiving, one his one hers

Call again Sojourner, my friend

We are done with hoeing cotton, we are done with hoeing corn;
We are colored Yankee soldiers as sure as you are born.
When massa hears us shouting, he will think 'tis Gabriel's horn,
As we go marching on.

Whipping posts
Linsey-woolsey dress tied up the legs
Melted fat drips scalding scalp
Starvation
Rape
Rough sex
Rough coffin
Bloodhounds
Rat eaten
Raw
Lashed, bound
Auction block
Ears boxed
Shackled, branded
Babes torn from mothers' breasts
Nipples torn from babes

As we go marching on
As we go marching on

Calamity Jane

Here, the season of manifest destiny
And breaded trees

Land-hungry time
Backstairs time

In each of us
An eyewitness

Marthy Cannary
By herself

An eyewitness

———

Born 1852, Missouri
oldest of six brats

rider until I became an expert rider,
able to ride the not-ridable
horses, which I spent
my early and later life riding

overland to Virginia City, five-month
journey, hunting the plains
or adventuring, shooting
and riding way beyond

many times crossed
the Rockies

to Montana, our wagons
lowered over ledges,
boggy places, no use
to be careful

lost all, horses and all,
then there were dangers,
streams swollen; mounted
a pony to swim through currents and save

lives or to amuse ourselves.
Narrow escapes. Simple escapades,
reached for obstacles and overcame
as God is witness.

At Blackfoot, Mother died;
I buried her under the spring.
She taught me weather,
strength, and to cuss. Then

To Salt Lake. Where my father dies.
Joined General and his campaign.
Between Deadwood and Custer
Molested very little.

Ordered out to the Muscle Shell
Or Nursey Pursey Battle; in saddle
Swirled to catch and cradle
Egan in my arms. Christened
Me Calamity, heroine.

To rely on what
One had once
Lost faith

Perseverance keeping
The quiet outer
Fact

Synchronicity and spirit

Doris Day is Calamity sipping sarsaparilli

Bill can't see her beauty till she drops
her coat, can't see her
face or coif. Or hear her
sing, "My gun got so hot had to sit
with a muzzle between my legs."
Her magic: pink chiffon.

Made into a woman

"no changeless essence... no eternal verities"

     Custer, Custer, elle était plus qu'une prostituée
a true star of gold
     ornée d'une étoile
la défroque of all *théâtre*
     tout le monde

Jane Russell and Jean Arthur,
John Wayne and Bogie too.
The frontier's Florence Nightingale.

Custer, she *was* more than a prostitute,
an *assassine-squaw*

First met up with her long about '75. Business was off so
rooming cottages built and ladies called for to occupy them.
They was of the sporting variety, would have to be wanna come
to Fort Laramie. Common like Jane. Her and some few others

followed General Crook and when General Merritt sent wagons back home the women rode with the wounded.

Tongue River

The gold rush was a period in American
history when men were digging and mining.

   Oremos, oremos
   angelitos somos,
   del cielo venemos
   a pidir oremos

of riches and respect, out of gulches
came jealousy, destruction of the unseen.

   ... we little angels
   from heaven come
   to ask for treats

selves, hearts, and emptiness

Spectral
War vets sit
Armless

Encrusted black
Marble
Plowshare

Hero infatuations
And Methodist
Prohibitions

Painted sex
Front-tier stage
Ghosting tips

Chartreuse plumes chanteuse.
Cheyenne. *Le chuk wagon.*
Young muscled whackers,
Triple-barreled and stallion-tailed

Deadwood, New Dakota
Derring-do boom
Gold Black Hills

From Kingdom Come
Calam & Wild Bill
Parade down Main

Donned in buckskin, in beaver,
hammered silver, the sun
children, five men

And Jane joins the pageantry
on horse, not prospector
but sentimentalist scout

The Queen with rosemary
potpourri and cowhands
never bedded sober
or pennies in her pocket

       to awaken on a familiar cot and recall
a fairy tale

"You're a wonderful little woman to have around in times
      of calamity,"
says Captain Egan when I save his life.

       To awaken in an unfamiliar fairy tale

Letters to your
self, inflammation of bowels
weaver and vowel lover

sense of restriction like touch

part of her
life nutrient

confessions encoded
in the photo-album
diary of a surface
wound

Your rest in her sleep

Master says, "With your eyes, what have you
Seen? With ears, what have you heard?
What have you said with your mouth?

As none of these was ever practiced

From where come such colors, sounds, and scents?"

Be not afeard. The isle is full of noises

Hat Creek
Calamity Peak
Drunk at Jack's Bar
Fell in a lake

Relationship with memory,
the dark star

"Deadwood Dick,
Rider of the Lugubrious Hills"
Disaster

(Now, isn't that rich)

Beautiful white devil of the Yellow
Stone, Heroine of Whoop-up,

In the melodramatic role
Calamity Jane she expounds

(Tight as a three-leg goat)

Billings, Montana, *Gazette*.
Daughter of Janie & Wild Will
Exclusive. Mother's secret diary.
Her confessions. Her letters.

The real Calamity Jane for one
      dime only

Her deeds and miscredits

Student asks, "Are clouds
running from or chasing the moon?"

"With your mind, what have you fathomed?" replies Master.

Basic fears never materialize
Wherever the body travels
Hometown strangers send it back

    of characters she once was

As in the Noh play, when the lover
Arrives at noon to find no reflection
Alive, she collects change of dreams

    after the lust is gone

They can meet in different parts

    previous world

Shadows lengthen
in anticipation of shades

Replace the word *power* with...
The costume of one's sex.
Passion for male clothes
and companionship
a paradox-mask.

"Pard we will meet again
in the Happy Hunting Ground
to part no more," the stone
        signature,
written, not in letters, but in her
where signatures of all things
can never be erased, ceased
the afterglow

gun

Imaginary

Hog ranch on the outskirts
Institute for Ladies and Gayeties

to accept her
sleep as his access to her pleasure

exhibit her
exclusively
cow-craft

Bill she thinks she is.
And discovers the cruelty
of identities, difference

Forces of air into peaceful
movements; sound
(gentle and
directional)
reveals
the deep
vertebral column

They weave sashes and blankets
Swap stories

migrations over imaginations

orchestrated

held in irons for that which they depend upon

one custodian must bear
the water jar

must gather
clay, shape, and fire

beside the power
behind the prayer of ocean

will draw water from the distant
moon without end

until the sky is dry
her eyes

witness
herself

A door above
your head left ajar
for the emergence

of far-off planets
echoing eloquence
toward bottom

They switch the date of death
to coincide with Bill's
and bury her by his side

Which animals befriend her?
the cat, the kite, the mule:
stubborn, hunter, stray

Le Diable Blanc
at the Number 10 Saloon
Mount Moriah

broken light and grasses
chilled in winter glass
a double sunset

*That you choose to destroy, but save
instead, is the purest act of Love.*

Madame Bubble

MERCY sings: Now then you hang there, and be a sign
To all who shall against the truth combine.
And let him who comes after, fear this end,
If unto pilgrims he is not a friend.

Bridget Bishop, wife of Edward Bishop of Salem
in the County of Essex, sawyer, at a special court
of Oyer and Terminer held at Salem the second
day of this instant month of June, eight of the
clock in the forenoon.

Hanged on Witches' Hill

MERCY sings: Now you must pay for all our sins.
You've kept to yourself without confessions.
And let him who comes after, fear this end,
If unto pilgrims he is not a friend.

Her legs were long, a broom
she carried herself where she wanted.

In a dream she raised her arm and disclosed
a hole in her heart plugged by sealing wax.

When it was taken out, the spot
wept. She held that pose before me

until I could look no more and so awakened.
He dreamt he killed her — Guilty for what

God doesn't touch with clarity. My desire
feeds me cake and ale. A most private

and secret place she withdraws
to nobody knows where. Groomed by Mrs.

Love-the-flesh, she allows the young in.
Behind her walls, laughter.

It is more fun than the tavern, and
those weak may enter.

Prithee where be the good neighbor in her afflicted and troubled self?
Weep and heed, Goodwife!

Arrested as Mercy is impatient

See, said she, these little chicks both look forward toward Heaven
                    this little chick broth cooks warm in the hearth

See she had a common call and
        a brooding note and
        obedient tones

Prithee Goody, why weep thy troubled self?

The mark of

Bridget  Bishop

and a seal

Tied, gagged, back-to-back,
Opprobrious language written
on Master and Goodwife's heads

A candle, hot and waning from her heat

MATTHEW: Why are the wick, and tallow, spent
to maintain the light of the candle?
PRUDENCE: To show that body and soul, and all,
should be at the service of, and spend
themselves to maintain in good condition,
that grace of God that is in us.

Fingerprints on Goodwife's chest

The grace that is in us

Never before had Wonn, Negro slave, who testifies
against Bridget Bishop, met her but he recognized her
guilt, her desire for the impossible.

She wore a black cloak and walked near a black man.
Her orchard was grand and she lived outside town.
Her skin was tanned and her legs were long.
I never saw her, could never see her.

I AM innocent to a witch.
I know not what a witch is.

How then do you know you are not one?

Testimony

Winter, about midnight, this deponent felt something between
his lips. At the foot of his bed sat Bishop or her shape...

... and the deponent's daughter suddenly screeched out and died.

The child in her cradle, erect like a candle. Lord's Day. Pined
away. Knew not her name before, now forever stamped on
memory: for that she is guilty.

Bridget atop my body (I endeavored to awaken my wife but
could not) and oppressed me so, a good neighbor advised I sleep
with my sword to strike her when she come again.

... about her fowl that invaded our garden. Shaped on my
stomach, could not resist, almost until day...

Her pig vanished into my room.

... a yellow bird in her bosom. Gave suckle to turtles then
kneeled before the black man. And bid I touch her book.

Sheep takes her death darkly
Sheep suffereth her skin
doth call you a sheep
bleed in sound, not in body
hold it in.

God called his sheep child. Bridget hers Christen.
She had one daughter named after the Son

On the Western side of Salem town

Where the sun fell down

Barren and rocky

A gash made into a gargoyle, a ghost after the youths
had passed out her gate to nobody knows where, so be it.

Complaint Against
Examination
Death Warrant Against
Execution

Pleads not guilty

Witchcraft Witnesses:

Mercy Lewis says, she is Guilty

Mr. Samuel Parris, says Guilty

Abigail Williams, Guilty

Mary Walcott, Guilty

Elizabeth Hubbard, she is Guilty

Nathaniel Ingersoll, Guilty

Thomas Putnam, Guilty

Ann Putnam, Guilty she is

William Bligh, she's Guilty

William Stacey, Bridget is Guilty

**Against the peace of our said Sovereign Lord and Lady
the King and Queen**

No legal government existed in Massachusetts. The administration of 1689 had been overthrown, and shackled prisoners awaited trial. Sir William Phips, new governor, arrived in Boston May of 1692 and there established the Court of Oyer and Terminer which heard the backlog of witchcraft cases. Bridget Bishop, the first to be sentenced to death.

I have taken the body of Bridget Bishop.

No relation appeared on her behalf.

MERCY sings: *In hell you fry but never die,*
              You stay awake all night and day.
              And let him who comes after, fear this end,
              If unto pilgrims he is not a friend.

About the Author

Martine Bellen is the author of two previous collections of poetry. Her book *Tales of Murasaki and Other Poems* won the National Poetry Series Award in 1997. Bellen is a senior editor at *Conjunctions*. She has received the Fund for Poetry Award, a fellowship from The New York Foundation for the Arts, and an Academy of American Poets Award. She currently lives in New York City.

The Chinese character for poetry is made up of two parts: "word" and "temple." It also serves as pressmark for Copper Canyon Press.

Founded in 1972, Copper Canyon Press remains dedicated to publishing poetry exclusively, from Nobel laureates to new and emerging authors. The press thrives with the generous patronage of readers, writers, booksellers, librarians, teachers, students, and funders — everyone who shares the conviction that poetry invigorates the language and sharpens our appreciation of the world.

PUBLISHER'S CIRCLE

Allen Foundation for the Arts
Elliott Bay Book Company
Mimi Gardner Gates
Jaech Family Fund
Lannan Foundation
Rhoady and Jeanne Marie Lee
Lila Wallace–Reader's Digest Fund
National Endowment for the Arts
Port Townsend Paper Company
U.S.–Mexico Fund for Culture
Emily Warn and Daj Oberg
Washington State Arts Commission
The Witter Bynner Foundation
Charles and Barbara Wright

For information and catalogs:

COPPER CANYON PRESS
Post Office Box 271
Port Townsend, Washington 98368
360/385-4925
poetry@coppercanyonpress.org
www.coppercanyonpress.org

The font used in this book is FF Acanthus Text,
designed by Akira Kobayashi after a
type specimen from 1788 by Henri Didot.
Interior design by Valerie Brewster, Scribe Typography.
Printed on archival-quality Glatfelter Author's Text
at McNaughton & Gunn.